# My Home Is My Castle

## *Beware Of The Dog!*

*MAINE-PATRIOT.com*
*3 Linnell Circle*
*Brunswick, Maine 04011*

*maine-patriot.com*

MY HOME IS MY CASTLE

# Emergency 911

**Stop the Foreclosure with a Question !**

The magic question that will debunk any Foreclosure is the following. Ask this question in court :

*"Should the one who funded the loan be the one who is repaid the money debt?"*

If the answer is "Yes" or "No," the bank must zero out the alleged debt on their fraudulently created none-existent loan.

No lawful loan was made by the Bank to the alleged (so-called) borrower.

All bankers, politicians and judges know this truth and they fear the wrath of the public should their dirty secret ever become known by a critical mass of the people that they have been defrauding for decades. Meaning the so-called "borrower".

Bankers will not answer this question in any courtroom in the world because they know that the "borrower" is the one who actually and lawfully funded the loan. They also know that the evidence of this fact can be found in the loan entries of the bank's bookkeeping, according to GAAP (Generally Accepted Accounting Principles). Two other questions :

*"Is the promissory note an asset of the bank?"*
*"Was the promissory deposited in a demand account in the borrower's name?"*

# My Home Is My Castle

## Contents

MY HOME IS MY CASTLE

*"Forgive us our debts, as we forgive our debtors."* — Matthew 6:12.

GOD BLESS AMERICA

# My Home Is My Castle

From time immemorial the home has been the most important factor in human society! It is at once the cradle of civilization — the foundation of society and the cement that binds and holds civilization and society together.

The highest ideal, the chief ambition of good American citizens, young or old, is to own their own home. The home is a man's castle. It should be inviolate from all intrusion. It should be placed beyond the reach of all danger and of every encroachment whether of private or public origin. It should be *exempt from attachment.*

Not even the government should be permitted to take a man's home away from him!

No nation rises above the conditions of its homes. Destroy the home, and by that act you destroy the nation.

Today, because of unemployment, thousands are daily losing their homes through foreclosures of mortgages and executions for debt and tax sales. And yet nothing is being done to prevent this wholesale destruction of the chief asset of the nation.

Is seems more important to some to declare a moratorium on banker's debts than it is to protect the homes of the nation by a similar *moratorium.* For shame on our great so-called humanitarian leaders who rant and rail about balancing budgets that they cannot even budget themselves, let alone balance; and can find no better way to get out of the dilemma that they themselves have precipitated than to propose *additional taxes* that can but sink the helpless taxpayer deeper in the treacherous quicksands of ever shifting taxation.

Just where is this insane policy ultimately leading us?

We have given the government the power to tax us, and that power, mind you, is the power to destroy. We look to the government to protect us, and suddenly we find it oppressing us by taking more of our property.

**This is nobody's fault but our own for we are the government.** And if we permit the government to run wild and pile up unreasonable expenses, we should expect the government to tax us to pay its bills.

Now the time has come to call a halt to this policy. We cannot permit the government and its banks to eat up our substance and our homes.

**Foreclosure helps no one,** not even the bankers themselves, who in most cases, not only find themselves with an unproductive piece of property on their hands but are confronted with the immediate necessity for additional expenditures for much needed repairs and improvements and the payment of current and delinquent taxes that have perhaps accumulated against these properties considerably under the sum for which they were bid in.

And yet, more than two million homes alone or farms have been taken away thusly from their helpless owners in recent years.

One insurance company has thusly foreclosed on more than one million acres of the best farm lands in the country and it is reported that one large banking institution has more than 7,000 homes and ranches on its hands which it has acquired by similar coercive tactics. Is it any wonder that the values of stocks are many per cent less than what they were before the market started on this **rampage of**

**wholesale foreclosures?**

The banks, the Insurance Companies, the Building and Loan Associations, and Mortgage and Trust Companies are loaded to the point of breaking with mortgages on homes and farms and other buildings. These mortgages constitute the bulk of the 'frozen assets' for which the government has been supposedly trying to help the banks unload upon the long-suffering but indignant tax-payer, while things are sufferable.

**What irony; what an insult to our intelligence!**

We permit the government to increase taxes to the point of confiscation. We permit private interests to deflate the currency **and withhold the credit of the nation** until the purchasing value of the dollar is driven down to the point where production costs far exceed the sale price of our products.

Then, when these same private interests expect us to pay a dollar obligation with a ten cent asset, and our labor will not produce the required number of dollars to pay the mortgage, we permit these same predator interests to foreclose on our lands and deprive us of our homes.

And as a final insult to our intelligence we permit the government to add insult to injury by bailing out these private institutions with money taken from us and which we again must cover (pay for) through taxation.

If by protecting the home we nurture disloyalty and discontent, then why is this not the most important thing for our law-makers to consider? What avails us if we bailout the bankers, to relieve their creditors, when we, at the same time permit the spectre of unemployment and poverty, low prices and foreclosures on homes, to destroy our nation from within?

I urge our Government leaders, first, **to declare a moratorium on debts that jeopardize the home** pending the present depression; second, **to take definite steps, through the extension of the homestead act to gradually, but permanently, make the home forever 'tax exempt and execution free!'**

This is not an unreasonable or revolutionary undertaking. It could be brought about in an orderly manner that will hurt no one. The benefits to be derived from such a program would be immense.

Home and farm mortgages have from time immemorial been considered the safest investments on earth. Could any security be devised that would even approach, from the standpoint of physical value and moral risk, the security that is offered by a farm or home loan?

Can it be successfully argued that the notes of a private banking institution, even when backed by the guarantee of the Government, which in itself has been shown to be in large measure dependent upon the security of its home owners, is superior to the security offered by the home?

Then why should the government not issue its own **'amortization free currency'** in sufficient quantity to absorb all the farm and home mortgages now in the hands of the Banks, Insurance Companies, Building and Loan Associations, and other similar financial institutions that are daily breaking under the strain of 'frozen assets' in the form of farm and home mortgages? **Instead of bailing out the banks!**

Such a course would be an advantage to everyone.

The finance houses that would exchange their frozen assets for **'amortization free currency'** would then be holding in their vaults legal tender paper in the place of their mortgages that now jeopardize their very existence.

The Government could refinance these short term mortgages that it would be holding in consideration for the issuance of its **'amortization free currency,'** into new loans running from 30 to 50 years, similar to those made by the Federal Land Bank, the only simony-pure, co-operative, borrower-owned financial institution in America, outside the realm of a few mutual Building and Loan Associations that have managed to escape the trap laid for them by the nefarious methods and legislation prompted by special privilege and crooked building and loan officials.

**Such a course would confiscate no man's property, it would summarily stop foreclosures and the attendant ruinous loss to creditor and debtor alike.** It would check the downward trend of realty values due to foreclosures. **It would put back into circulation several billions of dollars that have been squeezed out of circulation by that hideous monster, the non-federal Federal Reserve Bank,** and it would automatically balance the budget which we hear so much about by adding billions to our national income from the **'amortization free currency'** thus put into circulation.

**I don't hear you, Mr. Banker.** The tragic wails of a hundred million destitute, poverty stricken, hungry, hopeless human beings, submerge into oblivion the most frantic protests you are able to muster, from the handful of human barnacles that threaten to sink our majestic Ship of State.

**I do not hear you, legislators;** who have a **'committee appointed for the purpose** of determining the policies best adapted to fit the currency needs of the nation, who thereby seek to avoid **the sacred responsibility of their office.**

MY HOME IS MY CASTLE

# The Foreclosure Event

The Foreclosure of one's home is one of the most tragic and criminal events that can happen in a person's and his family's lifetime. The impending loss of a home can and does destroy the lives of those who are being foreclosed upon.

The process of foreclosure is designed to belittle and strip the dignity of each person in the family. The process relies upon unreasonable demands by the banks in their requirements and demands that are almost impossible to fulfill. The process is cold and unforgiving and does not give any thought of compassion or kindness to human beings. The process is designed to take the property as quickly and as quietly as possible from the people who have worked hard and honorably in trying to fulfill their perceived responsibility.

The banks count on these acts of so-called 'honor' in order to steal the property of those who are having a tough time in paying for the alleged "loan" they committed themselves to . . . all the while being themselves dishonorable.

Having combated the banks in the foreclosure process myself, I have learned by experience how callous and deceptive the banks are and how far they will go to foreclose on a property only to resell it again and do the same thing over and over again. The actions of the banks are deliberate, and only for creating more wealth for their owners and themselves.

We hope by writing this book that others will be able to

protect themselves from the foreclosure monster that is attacking the well being of America.

As of this writing foreclosures are happening in this nation at the rate of 150,000 a month. This is absolutely incredible. Even the Federal Reserve, the main culprit behind the confiscation of America's property, is very concerned because of the many foreclosures that are in progress. This could eventually lead to the altering of the banking system and the removal of their power as well as a transformation of government.

There is good news, however, if you are faced with the prospect of foreclosure.

The laws that the banks and Congress have tried to keep hidden over the last almost 90 years are coming out and becoming known. There are legal remedies that can save your home and free you from the slavery that the banks and the UNITED STATES, INC. want to keep you in.

We repeat:

There are legal remedies that can save your home and free you from the slavery that the banks and the UNITED STATES, INC., want to keep you in.

It is our hope that this information will start you on a path of knowledge and discovery and will help you be free — and free of debt as well. This is not necessarily a cure for those in foreclosure. It is a series of steps that can give you breathing room against the banks' deception so that you can learn how to defend yourself and challenge their legal authority to foreclose. The banks actually don't have the legal authority to foreclose and when challenged correctly they have to go away and leave you alone. When that happens, you owe nothing to them, and totally own your own home.

Do not forget:

The banks do NOT have the legal authority to foreclose on your home when challenged correctly, and they have to go away. When they finally do go away you will owe nothing to them and will totally own your home free and clear.

In this book we will give you areas to research so that you will gain a better understanding as to what is actually going on.

Everything in this book will be verifiable from one source or another and will allow you to be a better negotiator when dealing with the banks and the courts.

Yes, we did say courts. You may be faced with either suing or being sued by the bank. It's not as scary as you may think. There are things you will be able to do that will win the day even when dealing with a dishonest judge, which some of them might tend to be. We won't go into much of that in this book. The purpose of this book is primarily for stopping a foreclosure on your property.

Please keep in mind that the Courts support the fraud in the banking system. It is the banking system's bread and butter and mainstay, and they will do whatever they need to in order to keep intact, their scheme to enslave the population.

But, don't be scared, don't let them bully you into releasing your property to them. They actually don't have much, if any, legal authority to take your property, unless you allow them to. It's their practice to trick you into allowing them to take your property. There are solutions through education, and this is a good first step.

*"I have unwittingly ruined my country… We have come to be one of the worst ruled, one of the most completely controlled, and dominated governments in the civilized world. No longer a government by free opinion, no longer a government by conviction and the vote of the majority, but a government by the opinion and duress of a small group of dominant men."* — past President, Woodrow Wilson.

# 1

# All Mortgages Are Fraudulent

**All mortgages are fraudulent. — Former owners will have recourse to sue for fraudulent foreclosures. Spread this far & wide! The whole industry could completely collapse!**

Due to the recent ruling by the Supreme Court, MERS is not the title holder (real party in interest) of any property and never was.

All mortgages past and present are therefore fraudulent! This has devastating repercussions for all of the loan industry, not just MERS, because there is no longer a chain of title. People who have, or have had mortgages or are being foreclosed on, or have been foreclosed on, now have an out. These people are now able to win in court and are having their mortgages settled and are keeping their homes, for the banks fear losing far more in class action suits!

Now California is getting in on the action and suing MERS for filing false recordings with the county recorders in every county in the state, since MERS started filings over 10 years ago!

At a fine of 5-10K a pop, this stands to create millions and possibly billions of dollars in penalties against MERS which will effectively bankrupt the fraudulent mortgage industry. This could mean that anyone with a mortgage will have it immediately settled and the current owners get the title free and clear no matter what balance they owe because fraud has no statute of limitations.

Former owners will have recourse to sue for fraudulent foreclosures. The resulting litigations will have the banks on their knees in no time flat. The whole industry could completely collapse. Only time will tell.

Let's see what happens next.

A real estate market that supposedly produced more wealth than any previous one in human history is now in a serious meltdown. According to the market research company, RealtyTrac, 2.8 million homeowners lost their properties to foreclosure in 2009, with millions more facing the same prospect this year 2010.

According to the Mortgage Bankers Association, one in four homeowners (25%) is "upside down" — owing more than the property is worth. This is leading some people simply to walk away from their homes. In many areas, this combination of factors is leading to further slumps in already-depressed real estate prices. But there is an even more fundamental problem that is just now making its presence known – one that will greatly help the deeply stressed homeowner by preventing foreclosure, once its implications are better understood:

Thanks to the institutional corruption of the mortgage lending system, nobody can reliably say who legitimately owes what to whom!

# 2
# Mortgage Treadmill Of Debt

It has always amazed me how little attention people pay to mortgages, even though mortgages constitute the *largest debt* most people will ever see, in their lifetimes.

Other than *interest rates* and *monthly payment amounts,* most people don't even give *mortgages* a second thought before they get on what I call the "mortgage treadmill" of debt; the process in which many people get *new* 30-year mortgages, by either refinancing the one they have, or by moving into another property. Every time this happens, you start over at the *first* month of 360 more months of payments.

When added all up, instead of making 30 years of payments on an original loan, you have 40, 50, or even 60 years of payments on *consecutive loans.* This is on top of the fact that *for the first several years of repayment,* about 80% of each monthly payment on a fixed interest rate loan is *pure interest,* with only about 20% being paid on the *principal.* So if someone has a $1200 monthly payment on a $200,000 loan at a 6% fixed rate of interest, about $1000 of that amount is *nothing but interest* for the first few years of repayment. The lenders love this. Wouldn't you?

But just *who are* these lenders?

Most people are familiar with the consumer side of mortgages. You search for a lender, make your application for a mortgage, supply reams of information if you're application is accepted, then sign, and initial, a blizzard of papers at closing, including a *loan/repayment note.*

Although most people don't realize it, this *loan/repayment note* is the most important of any document they may ever have signed. Whoever owns this note is the party actually entitled *to receive the payments on the loan.* So what happens on the other side of the transaction?

What many people don't know is that within hours (or a few days at most) the mortgage you took out from the lender, or broker, is sold to someone else! That's right — sold! And the market for these documents is huge: Just enter the search term "mortgage note" into any internet search engine (Google, Yahoo, or Bing) and see the results you get.

In most cases, the mortgage will change hands several times before it settles down with a company that may want to keep it. For every mortgage sale that occurs, the *new mortgage owner* is supposed to record a *new/amended trust deed* (or lien) in the local property records. Also, although the new owner is required by the federal Truth In Lending Act to notify the *mortgagor* (the one who owes the payments) of the *change* in mortgage ownership, they usually don't. This makes determining an actual *mortgage note owner* complicated enough.

But things get even more complicated when you add the *mortgage service companies* into the mix. Most lenders use a *mortgage servicing company* to collect payments and do other administrative tasks.

Ever wonder why the company you make your payments to changed a few times, especially during the first 18 months of the mortgage? Most people don't even question why. It is usually because the mortgage was sold, and the *new owner* uses a different servicing company. So over recent years, determining who the mortgage "owner" is has become increasingly difficult, and sometimes impossible.

The first reason for this is a company called **"Mortgage Electronic Registration Systems"** (MERS). This is a Florida based company established by the major institutional lenders and banks. The main purpose of MERS is to allow its members to use its name as a *'nominee' mortgage owner* in local property records so mortgage sales among the members won't require any *new recordings* in those records to reflect a change in mortgage ownership. It saves a lot of recording hassles and fees. But, at the same time, it also makes a *mystery* of an actual mortgage owner.

The second reason is that during the mid-1900's there was more going on in the mortgage industry than allowing anyone who had a pulse, and the ability to sign a name, to get a mortgage.

Mortgages were bundled by the hundreds or thousands into blocks, which were then sold to investors around the world as securities. Investors could then *buy an interest* in one or more of these "securitized" mortgage bundles. But in the bundling process, an interesting thing happened — *many of the mortgage notes were lost or destroyed!*

For the few people who know about this, the fallout is just getting started. Over the last 2-3 years many people have successfully used this issue to defend against *the most dreaded lender hammer available — foreclosure!*

A news article describes the sentiments of Ray Garcia, a Florida attorney representing Ana Fernandez in her foreclosure proceedings. Chevy Chase Bank allegedly bought Fernandez's loan from another institution. Garcia says, when he examined the copy, it showed ownership of the loan *had never been assigned or transferred* to Chevy

Chase. *"As we sit here today, they haven't produced a note,"* relates Fernandez. *"They've produced absolutely no record evidence that Chevy Chase has a right to bring this action."*

Lawyer *April Charney,* who works with Jacksonville Legal Services in Florida, has become an expert on defending homeowners against foreclosures. She says *"asking the bank to produce the paperwork is just the beginning." "Lawyers who take the time to study the mortgage notes and the securitization agreements will almost always find deficiencies, and sometimes fraud." "These loans are so tricked up by the Ponzi scheme — the world of securitization and derivatives — that <u>there is no owner to these loans</u>!"*

What does all this mean to the average mortgage debtor? Without some *identifiable ownership* of a mortgage note, exactly who (if anyone) has the right even to receive your mortgage payments — much less bring a foreclosure action? If there is *'no owner'* for many of the mortgage notes, then you might as well be making your payments to your mail carrier, dog catcher, or local street bum. They have as much right to receive payments as any other *"non-owner"* of a note!

These circumstances will undoubtedly have a serious impact not only on foreclosures, but also with "underwater" properties, and mortgages in general. Isn't it ironic that the seeds for potentially ending the current real estate calamity are in the very instruments that significantly contributed to it — *mortgages?*

# 3
# Mortgage Scam 911

"Modern Banking" was created in Babylon over 4,000 years ago without the means of the electronic information we have today.

The *lending techniques* that are used today are diabolical, to say the very least. It took some very conniving people to figure out how to *appear* to be lending money when actually having the value supplied by the person wanting the loan. And this is what is happening today.

If you're an honest, ethical person who believes that *the party who funds a loan should be repaid,* then you can be helped. You will be quite surprised when you discover the truth.

All that we ask is for *equal protection under the law* and the bank's loan agreement that you signed, and for the *whole truth* about the bank's loan agreement to be revealed. This *whole truth* is NEVER revealed to the borrower. The bank (the lending institution) does NOT disclose to the public that *a Promissory Note becomes an asset of the bank* the moment you sign it; that they deposit in the bank, as their funds.

The bank does not tell you that *a Promissory Note is a "negotiable instrument" according to the Uniform Commercial Code;* that the bank will deposit, in the bank, to fund your loan. Nor that *the bank has a liability to you of nearly the same amount of the loan. By their own bookkeeping entries, according to GAAP (Generally Accepted Accounting Principles), the bank then owes* YOU *nearly the same amount of the loan.*

The bank does not *tell* you, that you in fact provided the actual value for your loan. The bank only *appears to be lending* you an asset of theirs.

That's right. Banks and lending institutions only *appear to lend money* to people.

Let's look at how money is created at the *government* level. Then we'll see how this applies to you and your alleged debt.

# 4
# How Money Is Created

The following steps will illustrate how money is created in the United States today.

1.  Congress decides that it needs $10 Billion dollars.
2.  Congress tells the U.S. Treasury that it needs $10 Billion dollars.
3.  Treasury prints up $10 Billion dollars in government Bonds.
4.  Treasury takes these Bonds over to the Federal Reserve Bank just down the road.
5.  Treasury walks into the FED with these Bonds and says, "We need to borrow $10 Billion dollars."
6.  The FED takes those $10 Billion dollar **"promises to pay"** that the printed Bonds represent, and in turn **"promise"** to loan the U.S. Government $10 Billion dollars in Federal Reserve Notes (fiat money). **One promise is exchanged for one other promise.**
7.  The FED writes into their ledger, by computer, "U.S. Owes us $10 Billion dollars."
8.  The FED then authorizes the U.S. Treasury to print the currency that Congress needs.
9.  Now the U.S. Government owes another $10 Billion dollars to the Federal Reserve, plus interest, guaranteed.

Government officials agree that this is how the banking system works today.

Representative Wright Patman, former Chairman of a House Banking Committee, said:

"The Federal Reserve Banks create money out of thin air with which to buy Government bonds. The Federal Reserve Bank is a total money and profit making machine."

When former Federal Reserve Bank Chairman Eccles was asked by Wright Patman, "Mr. Eccles, how did you get the money to buy these two billion dollars worth of government bonds?" Mr. Eccles replied, "We created it." Rep. Patman then asked, "Out of what?" Mr. Eccles replied, "Out of our right to issue credit money."

Former Congress Louis McFadden, former Chairman of the House Committee on Banking and Currency, remarked about the Federal Reserve Bank:

"The FED is a super-state controlled by international bankers and international industrialists acting together to enslave the world for their own pleasure."

When the unconstitutional Federal Reserve Act was about to be passed in 1913, Congressman Charles Lindbergh said:

"This Act establishes the most gigantic trust on Earth. When the President signs this bill, the invisible government by the monetary power will be legalized. The people may not know it immediately, but the day of reckoning is only a few years away. The worst legislative crime of the ages is perpetrated by this banking bill."

If you're an honest, ethical person, then you know and

believe that **all lenders should be repaid.** If the Federal Reserve Banking System repaid the value of the bonds it received from the U.S. Government, the U.S. "national debt" to the Federal Reserve Bank would be cancelled.

Let's Take a Quick Look At That . . .

In the example just mentioned, the bonds printed by the Treasury have an actual value of $10 Billion dollars. They take $10 Billion dollars in Bonds, over to the Fed, to "borrow" $10 Billion dollars!

An asset is anything that can be sold for money which can be deposited into a bank. Therefore, nothing of substance was actually loaned to the U.S. Government by the Federal Reserve Bank.

The Government took printed Bonds that could be sold for $10 Billion dollars and exchanged them for $10 Billion dollars worth of Federal Reserve Notes. Where was the loan? There was none. The FED and the Government made an *equal exchange,* but the Government and the FED call the *equal exchange* a "loan" — a label that is a lie which constitutes fraud.

### WHERE'S THE PROOF

We don't expect you to believe this without proof. This is all documented in the book, *The Creature from Jekyll Island,* by G. Edward Griffin. Mr. Griffin is a well-respected authority on the creation of the Federal Reserve Banking System and how it affects the money supply.

MY HOME IS MY CASTLE

# 5
# How This Applies To You

On a national level we see the absurdity behind the **"money creation"** process. But when it is here in our face it is harder to "see the forest for the trees."

Money is created on a local level through the banks and other lending institutions in much the same way. The value is first given to the bank by way of **your promise to pay** (your asset, your promissory note), the bank deposits the asset you give to the bank as the value that funds the bank's "loan" to you.

We know that this sounds absurd, but it's true. How can they get away with this, you ask? We wondered the same thing when we first uncovered this information.

The Federal Reserve Bank of Chicago came out with a very revealing publication back in the 1990s called *Modern Money Mechanics*. While this file is on a web page its physical publication on page 6 gives the exact mechanics of this, including bookkeeping entries.

So how does the bank loan actually work?
1. You want a loan for your home.
2. The bank advertises that they loan money.
3. You "apply" for a "loan."
4. They put you through the ringer and make you thankful and relieved that you were *approved* for a loan. (*You know, like they are doing you a really big favor*).
5. And lastly, they have you sign a Promissory Note.
HERE'S WHAT YOU'RE NEVER SUPPOSED TO KNOW

Since your promissory note can be sold for money *it is an asset just like cash.* The bank deposits your promissory note into an account *listed in your name* for the amount on the note less a few bank charges. The bank then cuts you a check from the deposit in your name that you never knew you had, or transfers the money to the people you want to receive it.

You think you owe money back on a loan *that you funded with your promissory note* when in fact the transaction was an *equal exchange.*

Now Let's Look At This . . .

If you stop to think about it, the bankers' scheme is brilliant! What other business can create money based on the value of a gift the customer gives to it, and then charge the customer for the amount he provided — plus interest to boot?

The real question becomes:

"If the promissory note is an asset to the bank what payed for bank's ownership?"

ANSWER: *The bank really does not own the note.*

You made an exchange. **Your promissory note** (*a new asset to the bank*) **for the amount of the loan.**

You gave the bank an asset worth $100,000 and the bank sold your promissory note to the Federal Reserve for $100,000 and gave the $100,000 proceeds of that sale to you as a so-called loan.

But was it a loan? Or a simple exchange? Where was the loan? There was no loan!

We have to admit, it's a brilliant scheme!

We're not the first people to discover that this was going on. A man named Tom Schauf initially researched this field. He's a CPA, who testified in court as an expert witness for nearly a decade. He taught thousands of CPAs across the nation how to be an expert witness in CPA Continuing Education courses. The information in his books is phenomenal. Everything is further explained and proven in his books.

As an honest ethical person who believes that all loans should be repaid, shouldn't the bank repay your loan of credit to them? After all, they deposited your promissory note as a bank asset in their bank, that they could sell and then exchanged that asset back to you calling the "exchange" a "loan from the bank to you" and expect you to pay the bank the value of that equal exchange, in payments of principal plus interest that you do not owe.

Your Promissory Note is an asset that they took in exchange for the Bank Check that they gave to you.

Where is the loan? There isn't one.

Since all lenders should be repaid, **the bank should repay the loan** they took from you via your promissory note. It should be a washout. You shouldn't have a *debt that you think you owe,* that you really don't owe.

When you deposit $100 into your checking account, doesn't the bank owe you that money back when you demand it? Yes. The bank has a *new asset,* the $100 you deposited into your checking account, and a *new liability* that says the bank owes you $100 when you want it.

(*Assets = Liabilities*).

The bookkeeping entries are the same for a deposit for

new loan as it is for a deposit into your checking account. By lending money the bank gains more assets and liabilities.

If you were to **lend** someone $500 your "pool of money" would become smaller; it would *decrease*. But when a bank **loans** money its "pool of money" becomes larger; it *increases* instead.

# 6
# How Banks Work

Money is created today by *lending.* All money is borrowed into existence as *debt money.*

The person who wants a loan must provide the bank with an instrument that he or she doesn't know is valuable to the bank. Your **signature** on a **promise to pay** creates the actual value of the promissory note.

A promissory note is a bank asset which the bank deposits into a demand deposit account. This asset gives the bank the value that it *lends* to you.

The bank exchanges *value* for *value,* just like our Government and the Federal Reserve Bank do, and then lies about it and calls it a *loan of credit* that it does not lend.

You and millions of others are led to believe you then have a debt. This is similar to counterfeiting, swindling and stealing.

Our founding fathers knew about this type of banking. This is why they made provisions in the Constitution of the united States of America to stop this system of banking from infecting our nation.

Article 1, Section 8, clause 5 states:

**"Congress shall have the power to coin money, regulate the value thereof, and of foreign coin, and fix the standard of weights and measures."**

Article 1, Section 10 in part states:

**"No State shall use any <u>Thing</u> but gold and silver Coin a Tender in Payment of Debts . . ."**

Banks create money with ***creative bookkeeping*** by depositing the value of your promissory note in a demand deposit account in your name and not telling you this. Whereas it takes ***labor and energy*** to mine gold and silver and mint money.

Mining is difficult and expensive, whereas Bookkeeping entries cost virtually nothing at all.

Take a look at the definition of **"Bank"** in the 4th Edition of Black's Law Dictionary:

BANK. An institution, of great value in the commercial world, empowered to receive deposits of money, to make loans, and to issue its promissory notes (*designed to circulate as money, and commonly called 'bank notes' or 'bank-bills,'*) or to perform any one or more of these functions.

A promissory note is designed to circulate as money and like money it can be deposited into a checking account.

This was never disclosed in the bank loan agreement.

The ***current*** banking system could not exist if gold and silver coin were our money. Our founding fathers knew this fact.

Since a promissory note is a negotiable instrument per the Uniform Commercial Code at what point did the bank obtain ***ownership*** of the promissory note? At what point did the bank get to ***own it?*** A note is an IOU which says, *"I owe you $X amount of money, a **sum certain** amount of money, which is to be repaid on this or that date or through* *payments."*

Did you give the bank permission to change your ***promise to pay*** into money? Very likely not.

When the bank ***altered*** your note and changed it into a ***negotiable instrument,*** they transferred more that twice the cost they received from you and all the risk to you. They more than doubled the cost to you by demanding payments, plus interest, and transferred all the risk to you by demanding ***collateral*** that they could seize for non-compliance with their terms.

You thought they were going to loan you ***their*** money or ***their depositors*** money before they deposited the note into a checking account. You thought that ***they*** were the ones at risk and that it was ***your duty*** to pay them for that risk.

When the bank deposited the Note in a demand deposit account in your name, the entire cost of the loan was funded by you — and you're now expected to pay them? That is not what you agreed to.

Because of this ***banking fraud*** you are in ***debt*** to the bank for ***money*** that you provided the value of in the first place.

There are ways to use the fraud committed by the banks to ***alleviate your so-called debt.***

There is no difference between the banking system of today and a thief who steals from you — or a counterfeiter who ***loans you counterfeit money*** that cost him nothing — or a con artist who swindles you into believing that you owe him money. There's no ***economic*** difference at all.

We live in a fictional commercial realm where ***there is no real money at all.*** All money is based upon ***promises***

***to pay*** — and not really paying at all — and when you understand the system and follow the system you can avoid it's ***intentionally designed*** pitfalls.

The Banker's Manifesto was exposed by US Congressman Charles A. Lindbergh, SR. (Minnesota), during his term of office (1907-17) as a warning to the citizens of America.

# 7
# The Bankers' Manifesto (1892)

The Banker's Manifesto was exposed by US Congress-man Charles A. Lindbergh, SR (Minnesota), during his term of office (1907-17) as a warning to the citizens of America.

*The Father and his famous son, Charles.*

"We (the bankers) must proceed with caution and guard every move made, for the lower order of people are already showing signs of restless commotion. Prudence will there-fore show a policy of apparently yielding to the popular will until our plans are so far consummated that we can declare our designs without fear of any organized resistance.

The Farmers Alliance and Knights of Labor organizations in the United States should be carefully watched by our trusted men, and we must take immediate steps to control these organizations in our interest or disrupt them.

At the coming Omaha Convention to be held July 4th (1892), our men must attend and direct its movement, or else there will be set on foot such antagonism to our designs as may require force to overcome. This at the present time would be premature. We are not yet ready for such a crisis. Capital must protect itself in every possible manner through combination (conspiracy) and legislation.

The courts must be called to our aid, debts must be collected, bonds and mortgages foreclosed as rapidly as possible.

**When through the process of the law, the common people have lost their homes, they will be more tractable and easily governed through the influence of the strong arm of the government applied to a central power of imperial wealth under the control of the leading financiers. People without homes will not quarrel with their leaders.**

History repeats itself in regular cycles. This truth is well known among our principal men who are engaged in forming an imperialism of the world. While they are doing this, the people must be kept in a state of political antagonism.

The question of tariff reform must be urged through the organization known as the Democratic Party, and the question of protection with the reciprocity must be forced to view through the Republican Party.

By thus dividing voters, we can get them to expand their energies in fighting over questions of no importance to us, except as teachers to the common herd. Thus, by discrete action, we can secure all that has been so generously planned and successfully accomplished."

## 8
# How Banks Process Their Loans

Without going into a lot of detail we are going to give a brief description of how the banks work when they make loans, and of promissory notes and Deeds of Trust.

You can do further research by reading **"Modern Money Mechanics"** published by the Federal Reserve in Chicago.

This is no longer being printed because it gave too much information on how banks create money, but you can access a copy over the Internet. The Chicago FED also published **"The Two Faces of Debt"** and **"Hats the Federal Reserve Wear"** which is also available.

The Federal Reserve in New York published **"The Story of Checks and Electronic Payments"** and The Federal Reserve in Philadelphia published **"A penny Saved"**.

Also read **"Creature from Jekyll Island"** by G. Edward Griffin. This book explains how the banking system has been manipulated to enslave the American population.

These publications tell exactly how the banks work and it will give you information on how to **challenge** the loan and the **illegal actions** of the banking community.

Different branches of the Federal Reserve print different books so you won't get the whole picture of what is going on in the banking world.

Banks act as *exchangers,* **exchanging security interests (promissory notes) for Federal Reserve Notes,** like exchanging Euro's of a particular exchange rate into Dollars of a different exchange rate. Banks are given *one form* of currency which they exchange for *another form.*

An exception to this illustration is the promissory note. Promissory notes are of the same exchange rate as Federal Reserve Notes.

When you want to buy a house (or anything else for that matter) you negotiate a price for the house that you want and go to the bank and ask for a loan with which to buy that house. Many things begin to happen at this point.

You fill out a loan application, and present documentation to support your application. Sometimes you pay fee's up front, or later when the fee's become part of the alleged loan.

You wait and get an approval for a loan on certain conditions established by the bank (and they can be very creative in what they ask of you). You decide to accept those conditions and meet at an attorney's office, or other place (such as an escrow company or title company) to close the deal by signing the documents involved.

The previous hoops the banks made you jump through are nothing but smoke and mirrors designed to trick you into thinking that you are actually getting a "loan" rather than making a *quid pro quo* (*equal value for equal value*) exchange.

**You're not getting a "loan". You are exchanging one *form* of security for another *form* of security**.

The banking system we use is also being used in Europe. Under this system, **the banks** (Federal Reserve member Banks) **are privately owned business corporations that do not loan out their depositors money**.

When the government needs cash, the Federal Reserve Bank buys its Federal Reserve Notes from the US Treasury at the cost of printing, paper, and ink, regardless of the denomination of the Notes. The Federal Reserve then uses these Federal Reserve Notes, that cost the FED next to nothing to have printed, to buy United States Bonds from the United States Government to be cashed back in at a later time when they mature.

The non-federal Federal Reserve Bank gets its money for fractions of a penny on the dollar and loans it to the US Government for outrageous amounts of interest while stealing the wealth of the people by charging for something they are getting practically for free.

Each the cost to the bank is getting less and less because we are becoming a paperless society. This is why banks are pushing credit cards, ATM cards, and wire transfers so hard. This is all done by ledger transfers where the cost of printing is zero.

The same concept applies for promissory notes and bonds, which leads us into the next chapter.

*"....You are a den of vipers. I intend to **wipe you out,** and by the Eternal God I will **rout you out**... If people only understood the rank injustice of the money and banking system, there would be a revolution by morning." — Andrew Jackson.*

*"Most Americans have no real understanding of the operation of the international money lenders. The accounts of the Federal Reserve System have never been audited. It operates outside the control of Congress and manipulates the credit of the United States" — Sen. Barry Goldwater (Rep. AR).*

*"The financial system has been turned over to the Federal Reserve Board. That Board administers the finance system by authority of a purely profiteering group.*

The system is **private,** conducted for the sole purpose of obtaining the greatest possible profits from the use of other people's money" — Charles A. Lindbergh Sr., 1923.

"The Federal Reserve bank buys government bonds without one penny..." — Congressman Wright Patman, Congressional Record, Sept. 30, 1941.

"We have, in this country, one of the most corrupt institutions the world has ever known. I refer to the Federal Reserve Board. This evil institution has impoverished the people of the United States and has practically bankrupted our government. It has done this through the corrupt practices of the moneyed vultures who control it". — Congressman Louis T. McFadden in 1932 (Rep. Pa).

# 9
# Signing The Promissory Note

OK, so you are now seated in the enemy's camp. You are probably sitting across from a person representing the Bank, the Escrow Company, the Title Company or the Loan Company. Someone who is a Notary. He or She brings out a stack of papers for you to sign. **You're actually suppose to read them first.** But usually the person across from you just wants to get through the process as quick as possible and gives you a brief description of what you are about to sign.

After seeing, initialing, and signing dozens of different papers including, disclosure statements, waivers, settlement statements, HUD documents, and many other papers you come to what is termed a **promissory note**, or **adjustable rate mortgage note,** or any number of papers ending with the word **Note** and having in it your promise to pay.

This document is usually 12 to 18 pages long with paragraph after paragraph of legal jargon that is enough to put any normal person to sleep after the first two pages. You are asked to place your initials in at least a dozen places and sign your name on the last page, just as you would a personal check.

In this document are the terms of the alleged loan, as well as the interest rate, and of course what they can do to you if you do not to pay back, or are late in paying the "money" they have supposedly lent you. Things like who the *Servicing Company* is and that they have the right *to sell the loan* to another party. It lists who the *Trustee* and *Beneficiary* are in case they have to foreclose on the loan. They are saying or implying that they will be holding the note and will return it upon *payment in full* of the loan. There are a lot of things in that document, but even more than that are **the things they are *not* disclosing** such as what they are actually going to do with that Note once you've signed it and have given it to them. **This is where the fraud really begins.**

We use the word *alleged* in talking about money and loans. **The fact is that they don't loan you money at all.**

There has not been any real "money of account" in this country since 1933 when Congress enacted HJR-192, on June 5, which removed gold and silver from the business economy of our nation.

We are no longer dealing with a money system backed by silver and gold. **We are using promissory notes**, such as Federal Reserve Notes (FRNs), **backed by the labor of the land,** which is **collateral** for the bankruptcy of the United States.

**Back to the promissory note that you signed.**

The promissory note that you signed is a one sided contract that **when you sign it you give your rights away to the bank in exchange for absolutely nothing.** Being a one sided contract (meaning, you were the only one who signed it) *gives you the legal option to change that contract if you discover that it is not working in your best interests.* The fact is that the promissory note you signed is probably **based on "non-disclosure," which voids any contract**.

**Nearly every promissory note written by a bank or finance company is based on deceit**.

Some of that deceit is:

1. Lack of consideration given in exchange for your promissory note.

2. Non-disclosure of all facts regarding the use of the promissory note and your signature.

3. Non-disclosure of monetizing the promissory note.

4. Non-disclosure of the bank's relationship to the trustee and beneficiary.

5. Non-disclosure of the bank's lack of authority to foreclose.

6. Forgery of document you gave to the bank for safekeeping.

This list goes on and on.

It is a deliberate practice of the financial institution to deceive you, and keep you an economic slave, to keep you paying the interest on the bank credit loaned to the bank by the IMF.

We recommend that you read the above-mentioned books and **USC Title 11 and 12.** "The bankruptcy laws."

The banking laws will amaze you as to what the law says that a bank **can** and **cannot do.**

Here is a brief summary of the numbered items above.

1. **Lack of consideration.** — All contracts must have consideration to be valid. The note you signed, which the bank monetized (turned into money) and deposited in their bank with no consideration to you. Your "exchange" was *a gift to them* and *a charge to you.* And in return for your *gift to them* you were given a bill (a charge) of the same amount which you had to pay on for 30 years including interest.

2. **Non- disclosure** of the use of the promissory note and your signature. — You were not told they were going to open an account in your name to monetize the note you signed.

3. **Non–disclosure** of the monetizing of the promissory note. — You were not told about the process of monetizing a security interest.

4. **Non–disclosure** of the banks relationship to the trustee and beneficiary. — Most banks own and control the **trustee** and **beneficiary** specified in the contract note. This is illegal and a conflict of interests. This makes the note in its present form void.

5. **Non–disclosure** of the bank's lack of authority to foreclose. — If you signed a note including a government form in it from HUD, it puts the loan under government regulations regarding the authority to foreclose. A bank cannot legally foreclose on a note if no **commissioner** has been appointed by HUD to oversee the foreclosure.

6. **Forgery** of the document you gave to them for safekeeping. — When the bank alters your promissory note in any way it's an act of forgery. A simple "For Deposit Only" on the back of the note is an act of forgery.

These are just a few of the things that banks and finance companies are doing to deceive the consumer in a definite pattern of unlawfulness.

**By law, the banks must give adequate and fair compensation to you for your promissory note.** And per law (12 USC 1813) they must give you a *deposit receipt* when they deposit your promissory note in their account establish in your name.

**Did you get one? Were you compensated for the promissory note, or just given a so-called loan**. Was it disclosed to you what they were going to do with your promissory note? All of this and much more can be challenged.

Please understand. In the promissory note that you signed is the phrase "for valuable consideration". This has been used in a court of law to say **the consideration they gave you was thought**. And you didn't object to it before you signed the note. This is the reason for filing an amended note. You must specify what the "valuable consideration" is to be.

*"Speaking the Truth in times of universal deceit is a revolutionary act." — George Orwell.*

*"Neither paper currency nor deposits have value as commodities, intrinsically, a 'dollar' bill is just a piece of paper. Deposits are merely book entries." — Modern Money Mechanics Workbook, Federal Reserve Bank of Chicago, 1975.*

*"The Federal Reserve system pays the U.S. Treasury $20.60 per thousand notes — a little over 2 cents each — without regard to the face value of the note. Federal Reserve Notes, incidentally, are the only type of currency now produced for circulation. They are printed exclusively by the Treasury's Bureau of Engraving and Printing, and the $20.60 per thousand price reflects the Bureau's full cost of production. Federal Reserve Notes are printed in*

*01, 02, 05, 10, 20, 50, and 100 dollar denominations only; notes of 500, 1000, 5000, and 10,000 denominations were last printed in 1945." — Donald J. Winn, Assistant to the Board of Governors of the non-federal Federal Reserve system.*

*"The regional Federal Reserve banks are not government agencies . . . but are independent, privately owned and locally controlled corporations." — Lewis v. United States, 680 F. 2d 1239 9th Circuit 1982.*

# 10
# RESPA
## Real Estate Settlement Procedures Act

**RESPA** — (15 USC Ch. 27 Sec. 2605) — was enacted by Congress in 1974 to stop the fraud that was going on against anyone involved with the act of making loans.
See: **http://tinyurl.com/2uq4jkt**

The very first thing we recommend is to send the lender a **RESPA request**. This puts the lender on notice that you think something in their behavior has not been appropriate. This is a very good tool because more often than not they will not answer it. Or they will give partial answers and say "I hope this satisfies your request". Which it won't. It's just a ploy to relieve them of any more responsibility.

**After 30 days**, send a **Notice of Fault with Opportunity to Cure** and when that is not answered send them a **Default Notice**.

Keep copies of these letters; they may be important in the future if you have to go to court. Also, send all mailings *"Certified, return receipt requested,"* with a **Declaration of Proof of Mailing** signed by someone who witnessed you putting the letter into the envelope and mailing it, or mailing it for you.

Pay attention particularly to § 2605. Notice that the Servicing companies *don't have legal authority*. It's all a bluff. But that bluff is supported by the courts, so at some point you may have to force a judge's hand.

*"The few who understand the system, will either be so interested from it's profits or so dependant on it's favors, that there will be no opposition from that class."* — Rothschild Brothers of London, 1863 (One of the owners of the Banks that make up the Federal Reserve).

*"Give me control of a nation's money and I care not who makes it's laws"* — Mayer Amschel Bauer Rothschild (One of bank owners that make up the Federal Reserved Banks).

*"Banks lend by creating **credit**. They create **the means of payment out of nothing**"* — Ralph M. Hawtrey, Secretary of the British Treasury.

*"It is well that the people of the nation do not understand our banking and monetary system, for if they did, I believe there would be a revolution before tomorrow morning."* — Henry Ford.

*"Banking was conceived in iniquity and was born in sin. The Bankers **own the earth**. Take it away from them, but leave them the power to create deposits, and with the flick of the pen they will create enough deposits to buy it back again. However, take it away from them, and all the great fortunes like mine will disappear and they ought to disappear, for this would be a happier and better world to live in. But, if you wish to remain the slaves of Bankers and pay the cost of your own slavery, let them continue to create deposits".* — SIR JOSIAH STAMP (President of the Bank of England in the 1920's, the second richest man in Britain)

# 11
# Before Default - The Steps

Here are the steps we would take if ever in the position of a **default on our home again**. These steps are taken into consideration when you know you are not going to be able to pay for the loan and a default is most likely in the future.

You can also use some of these steps to protect yourself in advance of any default or foreclosure action.

1. File with the State a "UCC-1 Financing statement" and "addendum."

2. File an "amended promissory note" with the County Recorders office. (notarized)

3. File a "Notice of Replacement of Trustee and Beneficiary." (notarized)

4. File a "Rescission of Power of Attorney." (notarized)

5. Send in a "RESPA request."

6. File a "UCC-3 amendment."

  a. Vested Interest, UCC-3

  b. Security Agreement, (notarized)

  c. Possessory lien. (notarized)

7. Send an "AFFIDAVIT OF TRUTH." (notarized)

Start educating yourself on the Rules of Court and the Rules of Civil Procedure.

## 1)  UCC-1 FINANCING STATEMENT

**The UCC-1 Financing Statement** can be found on your Secretary Of State's web site. Get familiar with the form and instructions.

And the UCC-3, and the UCC-11 too.

Do a UCC-11 search on your name to see if there is any claim against you.

The UCC-3 is an addendum that you can file at a later date to add more information.

You can also file another UCC-1 referring to the number of the original filing before you send it in.

The UCC Financing statement is used to give notice that there is a legal separation between you (the flesh and blood woman or man) and the fictional "person" (The fictional "strawman") having your name in all CAPITAL letters. Your real name is in *cursive* (upper and lower letters).

For instance, **PETER P. PRINCIPLE** is the fictional corporate entity, person strawman, and **Peter Paul Principle** is the flesh and blood man. If you look at your bank statements, tax returns and any *official document* you'll see it's in all capital letters, meaning a corporate entity.

A corporate entity can only do business (interact) with a corporate entity (**like kind with like kind**).

A corporate entity (like a bank, or the IRS, the government itself) can only do business with the **corporate you** — (your strawman) — not with the *living you.*

## 2)  FILING AN AMENDED PROMISSORY NOTE (notarized)

**Anyone can amend their promissory note** that they originally signed with the bank, because it is a one sided contract that only you signed. So you can change the terms of the note. Things like, interest, length of payments, late fee's, disclosure requirements, insurance requirements, property tax requirements and so much more.

Take a copy of your promissory note that you originally signed and start going through it, line by line, and start making notes on the parts that are not fair, or in your best interests.

## 3) REPLACING TRUSTEE AND BENEFICIARY (notarized)

**Replacing the Trustee and Beneficiary is critical** to the success of slowing down and even permanently stopping a foreclosure. The *trustee* and the *beneficiary* are key players in the foreclosure.

*The trustee* is given the power to foreclose and to sell your home at a trustee's sale or to give the task to the Sheriff. If you change the trustee to someone you can trust, the bank cannot foreclose on your home without your trusted "trustee's" permission.

Usually, the trustee that the bank puts in the promissory note is a subsidiary (friend) of the bank. (This is against Federal Law, title 12). The banks have gotten so arrogant in their belief that no one will challenge them that they do this with a blatant disregard of the law.

*The beneficiary* is the only one who can change the trustee, which is what happens. When the bank decides to foreclose they have *their beneficiary* appoint a new trustee who specializes in selling (stealing) people's homes.

This trustee is associated closely with the bank and does what the bank orders. If the trustee is *changed* to someone you trust and is actually interested in protecting you, then the bank will not be able to foreclose on your home *without just cause.* And the banks have *no just cause to foreclose,* because they have no legal authority to do so.

When the beneficiary is changed to someone you trust the bank cannot change who the beneficiary is because you are in control.

## 4) RESCISSION OF POWER OF ATTORNEY (notarized)

**Filing this document is also important.** Somewhere in your promissory note it is stated that you are giving the bank, trustee and/or beneficiary a specific power of attorney. You must rescind this so they cannot appoint someone else who will act in their best interests. A sample of this notice can be found in the documents chapter.

## 5) THE RESPA REQUEST

**An important document you must send at the very beginning.** They usually won't answer it or will try to appease you by sending some very vague answers at best or say they cannot answer those questions.

**This Real Estate Settlement Procedures Act** is a law passed by Congress to protect consumers from *predatory lending practices.* Title 15 of the USC is something you should read. The RESPA request asks the lender certain pertinent questions that puts the lender in a position of having to tell the truth and if he doesn't, and doesn't disclose what is requested, then he is in dishonor and default of a legal obligation. This could be used as evidence in a court of law, if necessary.

## 6) THE UCC- 3 AMENDMENT  (notarized)

**6.a) Vested Interest** — The vested interest statement gives notice that you have a priority interest and lien in the property that must be paid before the property can be sold.

**6.b) Security Agreement** — The Security Agreement is an agreement between the living person and the fictitious corporate person giving the living person control of all interests the corporate person has. This includes loans, contracts and the like. This agreement allows the living person to discharge the debts of the corporate person.

**6.c) Possessory Lien** — There are many different types of liens you can put against your property. The possessory Lien is just one of them, a mechanics lien is another. This is just one more way of protecting your property. We personally haven't used this method but may do so in the future.

## 7) THE AFFIDAVIT OF TRUTH (notarized)
The affidavit of truth is one of the most potent weapons you can use. When made out properly *and witnessed by a notary* it carries great weight in a court of law. It is also a poison pill in an admiralty court if the respondent does not answer the charges point by point. They are essentially agreeing to the truth of the document and by tacit agreement agreeing to what has been said in the affidavit.

## ACTION
You should be able to file and send all the above documents within just a few days (except for UCC3 amendments that are not required at this time).

**It is extremely important that you send copies to all interested parties** as soon as possible **by "certified mail, return receipt requested."**

## TIME IS OF THE ESSENCE

Time is of the essence in everything you do concerning this matter. After you send this information off you will want to make regular calls to the company who is selling your home to make sure the sale is being forestalled.

# 12

# After Default - The Steps

OK, so here you are with a default notice taped to your door and also received in the mail. **All is not lost** even if you have ignored the notices and you're 30 days (or less) away from the actual trustee's sale.

If you have but a limited time left then consider filing for protection under Chapter 13 of the Bankruptcy Act. This is an automatic short-term stay on the sale of your home.

While this stay is in place there are a number of things you will need to do in short order.

The steps in the previous chapter will for the most part also apply here, and you will have to act quickly for them to have the desired effect.

What you need to do depends on the amount of time you have left before the sale.

Let's say you just received the Notice of Default and you have about 90 days + 20 more until the sale. This should give you enough time to get all the papers sent off and filed. If it's fewer than 30 days you can start the paper work but you may want to file for bankruptcy protection.

**The immediate steps you need to take are listed in this order:**

1. File a **Notice of Replacement of Beneficiary and Trustee. (notarized)**
2. File a **Rescission of Power of Attorney. (notarized)**
3. Send in a **RESPA request.**

4. File a **UCC-1 Financing statement and addendum** with the State .

5. Send an **AFFIDAVIT OF TRUTH. (notarized)**

6. File an **Amended Promissory Note (notarized)** with the County Recorders office.

7. File the UCC-3 amendments. (After you have received the Original back from the Sec. of State) a vested Interest.

8. **Security Agreement, (notarized)**

9. **Promissory Lien (notarized)** and if the county recorder won't record it then file it with the Sec. of State via a UCC-3 Form)

All the above documents should be ready to file and send out in just a few days, except for the UCC-3 amendments.

It is extremely important that you **send copies to all interested parties as soon as possible by "certified mail return receipt requested."**

## TIME IS OF THE ESSENCE

Time is of the essence in everything you do concerning this matter. After you send this information off you will want to make regular calls to the company who is selling your home, to make sure the sale is being forestalled.

# 13
# Bankruptcy Court

The U.S. Bankruptcy Court is a strange beast. It can help you by giving you time to re-organize your debts while allowing the creditors to have a stronger stranglehold on your freedoms and life. All Courts in the United States are pledged to protect the Receivership of the bankruptcy of the United States. That means is that they are not your friend and they will do what is in the best interest of the corporate United States. This is because **Corporate America uses the American people to pay the costs of the bankruptcy**.

Some things to give thought to when you are ready to file for CHAPTER 13. (note, Chapter 7 is quite different and you might possibly lose your home) We personally recommend that you don't use an attorney. They probably are not working in and for your best interest. They are there working for the Banks, Courts, and finally their best interests. What they do is charge from 1 to 10 thousand dollars to file for you and represent you in court. Plus the filing costs. Filing costs are only a few hundred dollars.

It might be better to use a service that just fills out the forms for you. Be careful though. **Make sure you read all the forms they type out for you and check for any mistakes**. *One of the forms is telling the court how much your can pay.* If this is incorrect then you are stuck with it and then you will have to start amending your paperwork and that is a pain to do.

When filling out the paperwork we have found it wise, when you list the bank, *to list them as an alleged creditor and show that you don't owe them any money.* The reason for this is that *you are disagreeing that you owe them anything.* Usually it will be the servicer of the loan who makes the claim (B-10 Form) and it will *be an act of fraud.* The penalty for this to the person who actually signs the form is up to $500,000 or 5 years in prison or both.

As you will read in Title 12 of the USC (United States Code) it will tell you that a servicer is just that, a servicer and will actually *have no legal authority to collect on a debt* nor foreclose on your home. You will also discover that the Secretary of HUD must appoint a commissioner in order for a home to be foreclosed upon.

**99% of homes that are foreclosed upon do not meet the basic fundamental laws regarding foreclosures**.

When filling out the paperwork for the bankruptcy keep in mind that *you will want to pay as little as possible to the court each month.* Each debt collector will have to file a B-10 form in order to make a claim. In reality *each of those claim forms is fraudulent* and constitutes fraud upon the court because they don't have the **original promissory note** and they need that to prove they have a claim.

Don't make the mistake one friend did by not paying the agreed upon amount. His Bankruptcy was dismissed and he had to start all over again and it took away the protection of the sale of his home. All is not lost at this point but it made the situation much more complicated.

What transpired up to that point was that the court ordered the Servicing Company to *bring in the original note* upon payment of the money to the court. If the money was paid timely, the servicer had to produce the original note. When they couldn't produce it, *there would be no debt owed.* Case Closed. No debt.

**Title 11 of the USC is the law that governs bankruptcy. Read it.**

Bankruptcy in itself is a fairly simple process with easily understandable principles.

The Rules of Court are another thing. If you decide to be a *pro per, pro se* or *sui juris* litigant then you must start to read these rules as well as the Federal Rules of Civil Procedure.

By defending yourself you will be allowed some leeway but don't count on it too much. Knowing the law is the best defense and offense. If you know the law then it just might allow you to be less educated on the rules and procedures and be given more latitude.

*"The Federal Reserve banks, while not part of the government, etc, etc..." — United States budget for 1991 and 1992 part 7, page 10.*

*"This [Federal Reserve Act] establishes the most gigantic trust on earth. When the President [Wilson] signs this bill, the invisible government of the monetary power will be legalized...the worst legislative crime of the ages is perpetrated by this banking and currency bill." — Charles A. Lindbergh, Sr. , 1913.*

*"These 12 corporations together cover the whole country and monopolize and use for private gain every dollar of the public currency..." — Mr. Crozier of Cincinnati, before Senate Banking and Currency Committee - 1913.*

*"Neither paper currency nor deposits have value as commodities, intrinsically, a 'dollar' bill is just a piece of paper. Deposits are merely book entries."* — Modern Money Mechanics Workbook, Federal Reserve Bank of Chicago, 1975.

14

# Foreclosure Fraud 101

HERE ARE 68 POINTS THAT ILLUSTRATE THE FRAUDULENT NATURE OF THE MORTGAGE SCAM AMERICAN HOME OWNERS ARE FACED WITH TODAY.

1.  The Fair Debt Collection Practices Act (FDCPA) codified at 15 USC 1692 stipulates that **a debt collector must validate an alleged debt by affidavit, oath or deposition and cease all collection activity until validation is provided.**

2.  Validation or verification is defined as **confirmation of correctness, truth, or authenticity of a claim** *"to assure good faith in averments of statement of party."* — Black's Law Dictionary, Sixth Edition, 1990.

3.  **A debt collector must swear true, correct, and complete that** *an exchange of valuable consideration has occurred that allows him to demand repayment.*

4.  On an alleged note dated 00/00/00 regarding loan 0000000000 (Servicing No. 0000000) under point **No. 1.** **"BORROWER'S PROMISE TO PAY"** the signer's promise to pay is stated in these words . . . **"In return for a LOAN, I promise to pay . . to the LENDER . ."**

NOTE THE FOLLOWING DEFINITIONS:

5.  **loan:** to lend some thing, esp. money.

6.  **borrow:** 1. to take some thing for temporary use. 2. to receive money with the understanding or agreement that the money is to be repaid, usu. with interest.

*Beware Of The Dog!* 65

7. The **five essential elements** of a lawful Note are:

  7.1. **signature of the *maker***, the lender;
  7.2. **signature of the *receiver***, the borrower;
  7.3. ***due date* or dates**;
  7.4. ***specific amount;***
  7.5. ***clear sentence of intent.***

8. **The signature of the *maker* is often missing from the note making the note illegal !** *See 7.1. above*

9. It was not the bank's money that bought the defendants their home. The defendants received no *valuable consideration* from the bank. The defendant's Promissory Note supplied the credit for the sale.

10. In return for the defendant's Promissory Note (the defendant's credit) the bank leased the defendant's credit back to him as rent for thirty years and holds the title to the property for having supplied nothing to the transaction at all.

11. The defendant's Promissory Note has been sold many times without his knowledge or consent although the defendant's Promissory Note still belongs to him.

12. In monetizing the borrower's Promissory Note through fractional reserve banking practices, the bank increased its wealth *by more than nine times the value of the Promissory Note* and still demands that the borrower pay the bank the principal of the Note plus interest on the credit that the borrower himself provided.

13. Americans have been engaged in commerce on a **"Promissory Note Standard"** (instead of a "Gold Standard") since 1933.

14.  Congress borrows Federal Reserve "Promissory Notes" from the private non-federal Federal Reserve Bank with bonds backed by the credit of the people of the United States.

15.  The credit that Congress borrows from the people of the United States is called *"the credit of the United States."*

16.  "Congress shall have power / to borrow money on the credit of the United States." —Article 1, Section 8, clause 2, U.S. Constitution.  (USC 1:8:2)

17.  Federal Reserve Notes represent the United States CORPORATION'S promise to pay interest to the Federal Reserve Bank on the alleged Notes that Congress could make and issue itself.

18.  The borrower's Promissory Note created the money that the lenders gave back to him as a so-called "loan."

19.  The Bill of Exchange that the bank gave the borrower (the bank check) was worth *more than nine times that dollar amount to the bank* when the borrower's promissory note was monetized on the discount exchange market and through fractional reserve banking practices.

20.  As a so-called "thank you" for the privilege of using the *alleged borrower's* Promissory Note to vastly increase the assets of the bank, bank officials expect the alleged borrower to pay back the non-loan that he received as *his own credit in changed form*, plus the interest he is expected to pay the bank on the non-loan over thirty years, which nearly multiplies the cost of the alleged mortgage to him by a factor of times three.

21.  In addition, the borrower pledged to the bank the collateral of the property that he had already paid for with his Promissory Note, should he default.

22.  There is no "contract" in the mortgage process from the beginning; a mortgage is not a contract — just as the Constitution of the United States is not a contract — they are "constitutums."

22.1.  A "constitutum" is 1. An agreement to pay another's existing debt or one's own. 2. The fixing of a day for the repayment of money owed. — Black's Law Dictionary, Seventh Edition, page 307.

22.2.  The Constitution of the United States is basically an agreement to pay the US Confederacy's existing debt to the British King. It obligated the Confederate Sates when they ratified it, to their existing debt to Britain's King George.

22.3.  A Mortgage is an alleged borrower's unilateral agreement to pay the so-called lender's obligation to himself (the borrower) for his Promissory Note (his application for the "loan" of some "THING" called "consideration") — which as the alleged borrower he signed under non-disclosure, false pretenses, and fraud.

23.  A contract requires two parties, an "offeror" and an "offeree" (an acceptor) who at the time of the contract's acceptance (its creation) agrees to be bound by the offeror's terms, as evidenced by the signatures of both parties to the contract.  (the offeror and offeree)

24.  Every mortgage lender intentionally obtains his customer's Promissory Note by non-disclosure, conceal-

ment, and suppression of the material fact that the alleged lender is not risking any of his own assets in the transaction, and that the *alleged lender* intentionally obtained the alleged borrower's Promissory Note (his credit exchange) by concerted action with full knowledge of the end results of his participation in fraud, larceny, and conspiracy to defraud, in contempt of the RICO Act.

25. The mortgage lender is NOT a party to the mortgage according to the laws of contract.

26. No principal or agent of the mortgage lender will sign an "alleged" mortgage contract because he knows that he, the mortgage lender, is not tendering any consideration to bind the transaction.

27. Having provided no consideration and having shown no *intention* to be a party to the contract by signing it, neither the mortgage lender nor any third party who may purchase the mortgage at a later date has any "standing" to enforce the terms of the mortgage. Therefore the so-called mortgage contract falls (fails) "for lack of consideration" and is void.

28. After obtaining the note, the non-authorized actions of the mortgage lender, regarding the applicant's Promissory Note, create the "implied obligation" for him to disclose the material facts of the transaction to the obligor of the note. (the one obliged to pay off the note).

29. If the mortgage were really a contract, the mortgage lender would have *tendered consideration* and have in his possession *the original unmarked and unaltered note* in order to enforce the contract or to sell the note.

30.  When the mortgage lender obtains the customer's Promissory Note without consideration, he commits *constructive fraud* by acts of concealment of the material facts.

31.  The acts of *concealment of the material facts* establish a "breach of contract" since the mortgage lender has the legal duty to act in good faith and disclose all of the material facts relative to the transaction.

32.  Having obtained the customer's Promissory Note *"by constructive fraud,"* the mortgage lender is not justified to enforce the contract by any *"implied consent"* on the part of the alleged borrower because true consent, expressed or implied, cannot be given under a cloud of non-disclosure, concealment, and suppression of the material facts, or a state of duress.

33.  The Sovereign is deceived by the use of "the mortgage fraud" into **"use by privilege"** of what he considers to be **"possession by right."**

34.  A contract is a living body of law; an agreement made between living people with their full knowledge and consent.

35.  The main issue in this case is the banking industry's *long time practice of "constructive fraud"* by breach of contract, nondisclosure of the material facts, and larceny.

36.  A mortgage lender must be a party to the mortgage according to the laws of contract in order for the contract to be enforced.

37.  The alleged lender didn't loan one cent of the bank's assets or its depositors funds!

38.  A bank loans nothing of substance as consideration

because the bank is forbidden by Federal Reserve regulations from loaning any assets of the bank or its depositors.

39.  The borrower is always the original source of the principle amount of any alleged loan by virtue of his "promise to pay" (his signature on his credit application and his Promissory Note) from which a negotiable instrument is generated ("credit money" per UCC 3-104) which the alleged lender converts into a different form (a cashier's check, bank draft, or account deposit) in accordance with the lending policies of the private Federal Reserve, which new form is then issued to the borrower as the so-called "loan".

40.  This "loan" is nothing more than accounting digits entered on the bank's computer pad without the borrower's knowledge and consent.

41.  So-called loans that end in default are simply charged off, i.e. discharged by a bookkeeping entry with no loss incurring to the bank or the bank's depositors.

42.  The bank has no risk in any loan transaction and therefore no valid claim because the bank only loans the customer his own credit back to him.

43.  Banks do not loan substance, only alleged credit, only good will and intent.

44.  The banking system of the New Deal is fraudulent by nature and cannot be made legitimate by a false affidavit.

45.  The only person who can validate a debt is the alleged borrower himself.

46.  The lender simply exchanges *cash value for cash value* and the borrower is charged for this equal exchange

as if it were a loan of money to him.

47.  The bank claims that the mortgage transaction is a so-called loan but it is a quid pro quo equal exchange deceptively called a loan.

48.  The evidence of this quid pro quo equal exchange is in the bookkeeping entries according to Generally Accepted Accounting Principles (GAAP).

49.  No cash value was paid by the bank for the borrower's Promissory Note; the borrower's Promissory Note funded the bank loan check that the borrower received.

50.  When a borrower gives the bank his Promissory Note it has a value equal to the loan check that the bank gives him in return.

51.  Who paid for the accused's Promissory Note? No one. Title to the Promissory Note still belongs to the alleged borrower.

52.  When a bank grants a so-called loan they are transferring the cash value of the alleged borrower's Promissory Note to themselves which is conversion theft.

53.  The bank did not loan one cent of the bank's money or its depositors funds to obtain the borrower's Promissory Note.

54.  The bank posted the alleged borrower's Promissory Note on its books as a deposit from the borrower to the bank and uses the credit it obtained from the alleged borrower via his Promissory Note to create the check-book money it gives to him as the so-called loan, and vastly increase the assets of the bank by a factor of at lease nine

times through fractional reserve techniques.

55.  The check-book money they tender to the borrower has an equal value of legal tender because his Promissory Note will be sold for legal tender cash.

56.  The bank uses the newly created check-book money to fund the bank loan check they give to the alleged borrower to be repaid to them at interest over time.

57.  "The practice of law cannot be licensed by a state or State." — *Schware v. Bd. of Examiners, 353 US 238, 239.*

58.  "The practice of law is an occupation of common right." — *Sims v. Aherns, 271 S.W. 720.*

59.  A promissory note is a negotiable instrument constructed in strict accordance with the Uniform Commercial Code.

60.  Debt is discharged upon tender of a promissory note whether accepted or rejected by the payee.

61.  A payment tendered and refused is paid in full meaning discharged.

62.  No body has any obligation to pay in Federal Reserve promissory notes.

63.  Promissory notes represent the holder's right to enforce the promise of the note against the United States.

64.  Notes are legal tender for everyone.

65.  Commercial Redemption is a legal administrative remedy provided by Congress via Public Policy HJR 192 of June 5, 1933.

66. The collective entity rule makes a distinction between natural persons naturally created by God and fictional persons created the State.

68. No "exchange of valuable consideration" (substance) has occurred in commerce since 1933.

# 15
## In Conclusion

THIS ISN'T REALLY A CONCLUSION. It's simply a final word on the subject of this book. **You have here the basic tools to help you put off the foreclosure that have worked for us**.

By no means is this a guarantee that it will work. It has and does work now. It may not work in a year from now but when that happens the technology that we and others are working on will. All the time we are uncovering process and remedies built into the law that alleviate the debt and wrongdoings of the banking industry.

**The truth is coming out slowly. We will prevail**.

**Ultimately, I we hope to present a REMEDY to pay for all your debts**. It is there in the form of **Public Law 73-10, HJR 192 of 1933**, and several other laws passed by Congress. The fact that there is actually no money in this Country and that the economy is completely based on **promissory notes backed by bonds that are backed by the labor force of the American People** means that we can pay for our alleged debts the same way the Government and banks do.

We are also creating a process for those who have actually lost their home can be reimbursed for their loss and damages awarded.

Again, I must tell you that we are not attorneys. Attorneys know a lot about Civil Procedure and Rules of Court. We don't. We do think, though, that they know much about actual law. The information in this book is our personal opinions.

We give this information for entertainment purposes only and this information is not to be construed as legal advice. For that you need to see one of those lawyer types.

We will leave you with this. **You are what you think and you create what you focus upon**. Your life is in your hands and if you don't like what's happening there then, it is up to you to change your habits or your thought.

Everything works out as you plan it on a day-to-day basis.

*"Some people think **Federal Reserve Banks** are institutions of the United States government, which they are not. They are **private credit monopolies** which prey upon the people of the United States for the benefit of themselves and their foreign swindlers" — Congressional Record 12595-12603.*

*— Louis T. McFadden, Chairman of the Committee on Banking and Currency (12 years) June 10, 1932.*

# Appendix

MY HOME IS MY CASTLE

# 16
# Historical Background

The Europeans who came to North America were "grub-staked" by others — most likely the East India Trading Company, and The Bank of England. It was a huge venture which required money to get it started. So, the "colonists" got their start with hard money loans, in the days of hard money.

Once the colonists were established, they incorporated in order to deal with the burden of the debt. The first incorporation was under the Articles of Confederation. The effect of the Articles was two fold. First, to protect the interests of the creditors. And second, to protect the assets of the colonists who were working to establish a new economy.

The Articles were found to be weak in dealing with international contracts and enforcement of Admiralty/ Maritime concerns. So the Articles were rolled into what was called the Constitution for the united States of America. The Constitution tied up the loose ends left by the Articles of Confederation.

Since the people were trying to stave off bankruptcy and preserve the fruits of their labors it is obvious that the Constitution operated as a Constitutum in a reorganization bankruptcy mode. And as such, the law forum that the national government was operating in had to be Admiralty. *Bankruptcy reorganization* exists in Admiralty, while *bankruptcy liquidation* exists in Common law.

Hence the *common* law was always repugnant to the national or federal government, while the *states* used the *common* law and liquidation.

So, there was this distinction for a while between the bankruptcies operated in the national government versus the state governments.

But then a glitch came along with the Constitution regarding the minting of money. The national government decided to stop using gold and silver for money, and hence stopped minting it, and even passed a law demanding all US citizens to turn in their gold, and once the gold was safely returned to the national government they passed a law making it illegal for US citizens to own gold.

This caused a commercial dilemma. If there was to be no money, how could the people carry on commerce?

Well, as a *substitute* for money, the government went to the Law Merchant law forum for the answer. So instead of *gold* for money, citizens would use what the merchants considered *"good as gold"* — Notes and Bills of Exchange, or what are now called *negotiable instruments.*

The Law Merchants had used Bills and Notes for centuries with success, therefore *their way* of accounting in trade and commerce was adopted for use by the citizens of the United States.

The US adopted the use of Notes and Bills of Exchange under the Negotiable Instruments Act of the 1800's. This eventually evolved into what we call the Uniform Commercial Code (UCC), the rules and regulations of the use of *bills and notes* instead of *silver and gold.*

With the *new* form of "money" came a new form of accounting, *double entry bookkeeping.* Double entry bookkeeping has to do with balancing of *credits and debits* to reach *equity,* or a zero balance.

The zero balance of double entry bookkeeping has become a stumbling block for many who do not understand that we are operating under this system of accounting. In other words, if it can be found by *double entry bookkeeping* that there is fairness and equity, every one is happy and we go about our way. If *double entry bookkeeping* shows that there is inequity then we have to make adjustments to restore fairness.

This change in *law forum,* and the *type of money* to be used in public commerce, took place in 1913. This was the year when the Federal Reserve Act was introduced, and since it was not *successfully protested* in 20 years, it was accepted under the *international law of proscription.*

With the Federal Reserve Act we had a change in government, and a change in commerce as well.

One of the most interesting things that occurred was the establishment of a *prepaid system.*

To have justice, a debt must be paid. And an *anticipated* debt can be *prepaid* and dealt with *after the fact.* Therefore, legislators ruled that *all public debt was  prepaid.*

But they never told the people about this change, but kept it hidden from them in a controlled way. The people who trusted the government to regulate their commerce in an honest way, were kept from the knowledge about how this New Deal really worked, and were consequently robbed by those in society who *did* understand how the system worked.

Once the government began to operate its fictions, *new* considerations had to be launched regarding sureties and bonds.

*Everything in Admiralty works on insurance.*

Insurance can be seen as a *future indemnity* against injury. In a *perfect* world we could do without insurance, but since we sometimes make mistakes, we have to give *assurance to others* that we will not harm them by what we do.

This *assurance,* or *insurance,* could be in the form of a *bond.* A bond is a *future indemnity* against injury. And with that bond we had to make a way to collect against it, in the form of a *surety guarantee.*

So all the People of the United States were transformed into an *association,* a trust for the mutual benefit of all concerned guaranteeing by pledge that *no member can require any other member to pay his debts.*

I forgive all members of the association *their debts* as they forgive me *my debts,* hence "consideration" is "forgiveness of debt" one to each other.

This "forgiveness of debt" results in taxable events, since *fore-giveness* is not *giveness.* When we do something *before it is required,* this presumes a *prepay.* So when we "forgive", the *"forgive"* part of the equation is contemplated *prior to the "give",* hence the *Remedy* was created before it was *required.*

So the question is … who provided the Remedy before it was actually required? And when we find out who did that, what do we owe to this Remedy's "creator"?

In theology we call it a "tithe" — but in commerce we call it "tax". In theology we pay *tithes* in *substance* — in commerce we pay *taxes* in *bookkeeping entries.*

In *reality,* our increase is in *substance,* but in *commerce* our increase is documented *on paper.*

So we pay in kind. We tithe *substance* to the Creator, and we tax *paper documents* to the State.

Let's go back to the 1933 era and take a look at what had gone on to set up this system of "forgiveness of debt." It is of key importance to understand the difference between a *shadow* and the *thing* which produces the shadow.

On our planet we receive *light from the sun* (the thing that gives life to everything upon the earth) *many miles away from us.* We don't see the light until it strikes a thing which it cannot pass through. As an example, when the light strikes our body, there it stops and is reflected off in another direction. But if you look in a direct line *away from the sun,* you will detect *the absence of light,* which is what we call a *shadow.* The shadow is the proof that there is something *between* the shadow and the "Source of Light", the sun. So, in a logical way, the *shadow* is the proof of the *substance,* and without the *reality of substance* no shadow can exist.

Since the 1933 era we have been dealing with a *shadow government.* We are dealing with the absence of light when we work with the fictional shadow government. That being the case, we know that when we are dealing with the fiction that we are not dealing with *substance,* but the *absence* of substance. So, if we introduce *substance* to the fiction there will be a problem.

In the fiction world, when it was determined to go to *"double entry bookkeeping"* and *"money of account"* (rather than money of exchange…substance), a *bond and surety* had to be put up to protect the creditors of the bankruptcy.

The bond that was put up was an *"umbrella bond"* or *"supersedeas bond"* that was created. That bond was the *guarantee* or *insurance policy* that a citizen would not have to pay a public debt with substance.

That guarantee is best embodied in HJR 192 of June 5, 1933, and codified elsewhere. HJR 192 of 1933 was the *"indemnity"* provided for any future liability. SINCE IT WAS THE GUARANTEE THAT A DEBT COULD NOT BE COLLECTED IN SUBSTANCE, IT (ITSELF) BECAME THE PAYMENT IN FACT.

Now that there is evidence of the bond, *the umbrella insurance policy,* one would naturally want to find what the surety for that bond would be. What is the guarantee for HJR 192 of 1933?  The surety for the bond cannot be found in the *shadow* of the fiction. It must be found in the *substance* that creates the shadow. The surety must be *the people* and the *products of the people* created by their labor. The birth certificate is the evidence that *surety has been pledged* for the *guarantee of the pledge*.

But here we have a duality: The people in the *private* domain are insuring *themselves* in the *public* domain.  The people are the *creditors,* or the *funders,* of all the public business and public production. All substance that is produced in the public domain has to be returned from out of the *shadow, fictional, public domain* to the people who are the *"original creditors"* of the *manufactured, public production produced.*

So, the money we are using in the public is *"money of account",* which represents the *prior agreement* of all the participants in the association we call "America" — *that we will abide by the "Lord's Prayer."*

Remember the disciples asked Jesus how to pray, and he taught them to pray, "forgive us this day our debts, as we forgive our debtors [their debts]." (Matt. 6:12). This shows that the debt in question was previously anticipated and a remedy created before the act of the debt.

So, commercially, this might read as, "Apply HJR 192 of 1933 this day to me, as I apply HJR 192 of 1933 this day to you." It's the same process, indeed.

### APPLICATION TO ACCEPTED FOR VALUE

So, how do we make some sense of this "accepted for value" thing that seems to be so popular today? How does it apply?

Well, since the men and women are the guarantee for the liability in the public by the act of accepting the benefit privilege of limited liability to the public debt, then it is *obvious* that the men and women are the *creditors* of the public or national bankruptcy.

The men and women are the SPONSORS OF THE CREDIT they obtain from the International bankers.

What has happened with the US, is that it has been operating in a bankruptcy re-organization called chapter 11. This is an interesting bankruptcy, in that in it the filer of the bankruptcy fills the role of trustee in the bankruptcy in the position of "debtor in possession". And if any creditor in the chapter 11 dishonors the bankruptcy, the debtor in possession, in his role as trustee, will liquidate the creditor by the amount of the dishonor, because the creditor has become delinquent — the creditor had the obligation to settle the matter with the debtor but refused to do so when so requested and became himself responsible for the debt.

SO…any request made by the "debtor in possession" to the creditor of the bankruptcy MUST BE ACCEPTED!!! If not, the creditor turns into a delinquent creditor and gets liquidated by the "debtor in possession." So, if on a certain day a debtor comes to the creditor and says, "forgive me this day my debts" and the creditor does not openly and freely forgive the debtor, then the Lord will call him to account for that insult on the "prepayment of debts." In theology we would call it *blasphemy against the Son of God,* and in commerce we would call it *a violation against public policy.* It would a dishonor of a benefit which has already been received and utilized by the person when they became a part of the association of citizens who became guarantees to one another that they would not hold one another accountable for any public liability.

Now lets talk about those public liabilities that we are required to fore-give.

Anything that can be shown as an entry on a double entry bookkeeping account would be a public liability, of course. If a certain matter cannot be ledgered in double entry accounting, it is then most likely a matter to be resolved in a private manner, and not in the public realm.

You can easily discern a public versus a private communication. The public request for adjustment will *always* come directly to the trust account shown by the title of the trust being styled in all capital letters, such as JOHN H. SMITH. This is a direct attempt to attach to the bond of the JOHN H. SMITH TRUST. This is, of course, a violation of public policy to attach a *future* liability by trying to avoid the *present* liability.

This is a typical explanation of how one greater debt is used as the insurance policy for a smaller debt. The bill represents some past liability, whereas the note — the promissory note — represents the present liability, and then the bond is the indemnity for some future undetermined liability.

So, a device or scheme has been devised to attach the bond of the trust, which is in fact the labor of the men and women who have put themselves up as surety for the national debt, is for a holder of a past obligation to try to go around the present liability, and go to the bond…the future.

In other words, instead of settling the thing in the here and now, the present, the attempt is made to enslave the surety in some future event by attaching the bond.

We prevent that by taking the "bill" sent to the "bond" holder, and drawing it back into the present, by "accepting" the bill " for value" and returning it tto the presenter for settlement. By doing this we defeat his attempt to attach it to the bond for a future liability.

So, here we have the basis of AFV. The question that immediately arises when we talk about AFV is what do we do when the presenter dishonors the AFV. Those remedies are available, and will be the subject of other discussions at a later time.


AFV  = Acceptance for Value:


See also:
*"Give Yourself Credit: Money Doesn't Grow On Trees"*
http://tinyurl.com/2epqjxw

MY HOME IS MY CASTLE

# 17
# Legal Fraud Exposed

Every legal action when one is brought before a court — i.e. traffic ticket; property dispute or permits; income tax; credit cards; bank loans; or anything else that government might dream up to charge you with in front of a court — is a legal action in an equity court, administrating commercial law, under a debtor-creditor law as the controlling law.

We have equity courts today but not equity courts as defined by the Constitution for the United States or any other legal document prior to 1938. All the courts of America were changed starting with the supreme Court decision *Erie v. Thompkins* in 1938.

This is a terrible fraud perpetrated on all Americans. The courts of today in the United States see only two classes of people: Debtors and Creditors. Debtors always lose; Creditors always win.

There were five years of Geneva conventions between 1928 and 1932. For five consecutive years from 1928 to 1932, the nations of the world met in Geneva Switzerland to institute a private Public Policy for the participating countries. The United States, Great Britain, France, Germany, Italy, Portugal and Spain, etc., all declared bankruptcy in 1930.

If you try to find any 1930 volume of the National Record, which contains the minutes of what happened, you will probably not find it. This volume has been pulled out of circulation and is very hard to find.

Franklin Delano Roosevelt was elected as President of the United States in 1932, after the close of the Geneva Conventions. Roosevelt's job was to establish and administer the bankruptcy that had been declared, two years earlier, in 1930.

The corporate United States needed a legal case on the books to set the stage for implementing and supporting the bankruptcy reorganization that began in 1930-1931. Roosevelt started right away with "The Bank Holiday" and proceeded to pull the people's gold out of circulation. That was the beginning of the Public Policy of the corporate United States: per Executive Orders 6073, 6102, 6111 & 6260, and a 1933 revision of the "Trading With The Enemy Act of 1917."

During 1933 and 1938 Roosevelt stacked the Supreme Court with his friends and increased the number of Justices from five to nine. The corporate United States needed a Supreme Court case that would support the bankruptcy.

Some of the justices tried to warn us that Roosevelt was tampering with the law, and with the courts. He was bringing in a new order — a new procedure for the law of the land.

The bankruptcy was by compact that the corporate government had with the corporate states. This compact tied the several corporate states to Washington, D.C., the headquarters of the Corporation named "The United States."

The original Union States created the Federal Government, however, the Federal Government took control of its "Creators," the States, in 1933. The Federal Government registered its trade names as: "United States"; "U.S."; "U.S.A."; "United States of America"; "Washington, D.C."; "District of Columbia"; "The Feds"; and "Federal Government". The Federal Government has its own U.S. Army, Navy,

Air Force, Marines, Parks, Post Office, etc., etc.

The United States gave its land, its personnel, and the money it takes from Americans via the IRS, and even its state franchise corporations, to the United Nations and the International Bankers, as payment for its debt.

The United Nations and the International Bankers use this money and services for various world wide projects, including War.

War is a very lucrative business for the New World Order United States, and the bankers, involving loans for destruction; and loans for reconstruction; and for controlling the people of the world.

# 18

# Roosevelt Stacks Supreme Court

The new players of the Supreme Court fully understood that they had to destroy all case law established prior to 1933. The statutes at large had to be perverted. They finally got their case in *Erie v. Thompkins,* in 1938. Right after that case the American Law Institute and the National Conference of Commissioners on Uniform State Laws began creating the Uniform Commercial Code that we have today.

Here is a direct quote from the preface of the official text of the 12th edition of the UCC:

"The Code was originally approved by its <u>Sponsors</u> and the <u>American Bar Association</u> in 1952 and was revised in 1958 to incorporate a number of changes that had been recommended by the <u>New York Law Revision Commission</u> and <u>other agencies</u>. Subsequent amendments that were deemed desirable in light of experience under the Code were approved by the <u>Permanent Editorial Board</u> in 1962 and in 1966."

The above named groups and associations of private lawyers got together and started working on the Uniform Commercial Code. By the early 1940's and during the war, this committee was working to form the UCC getting it ready to be published and put to work.

The UCC is Law Merchant Code for administering the Bankruptcy. The UCC is now the law of the land as far as the courts are concerned. This legal Committee of Lawyers put everything under the UCC.

By the middle of the 1960's, every state had passed the UCC into law. The states had no choice but to adopt the newly established Uniform Commercial Code as the law of the land. The states had to administer the bankruptcy.

Washington, D.C. adopted the Uniform Commercial Code six weeks after President Kennedy was assassinated in 1963.

**Since *Erie v. Thomkins* (1938) no court cases can be cited prior to 1938.** There can be no mixing of old case law with the new.

The members of the American Bar Association, controlled by the Lawyer's guild of Great Britain, established and implemented the new bankruptcy law. The American Bar Association is a franchise of the foreign Lawyers Guild of Great Britain.

Since the *Erie v. Thomkins* was decided, it has been reported, every lawyer has to take a confidential oath to support the bankruptcy.

As Officers of the Court they have sworn to uphold the law as it exists, commercially, today, just as they have been taught. The lawyers and judges promise never to reveal who the Creditor is in the bankruptcy proceedings, if, indeed, they even know.

If there is no appearance of the **"true party to the action"**, there is no way the defendant can know the **"true nature and cause of the action"** against him. You are never told the **"true nature and cause"** of why you are in front of their private court. The court is forbidden to tell you this information.

If you question the **"true nature and cause"**, the judge will say, *"It's not my job to tell you that. I can't give you legal advice from the bench. I suggest you hire a lawyer."*

The problem you have is this, if you hire a lawyer who is pledged not to reveal the **"true nature and cause"**, you can never find that out.

If the **"true nature and cause of the action"** against you were revealed, it would expose the real Creditor from whom this action and cause came. They would have to name the true Creditor, and the true Creditor would have to take the stand and state that the **"nature and the cause of the action"** against you is a bankruptcy proceeding. The true Creditor would have to say, "I'm the Creditor and he's the Debtor."

Such a declaration would open the door to this question: *"Who in the world are you?" How did I promise to become a debtor to you?"*

The courts on every level are administrating the Bankruptcy and are pledged not to reveal who the true Creditor is, and how the defendant became pledged as a debtor to "Him" — to the World Bank and the IMF (the International Monetary Fund) for the Federal National Debt.

What would really do away with these people would be to compel the International Bankers to send a lawyer into the courtroom and present himself as the attorney for the **"true creditor"**, the International Bankers and the IMF, then have that attorney put into the record the **"true nature and cause"** of the proceeding against the defendant on that particular day.

The International Bankers told these people that the people were in a state of bankruptcy. Their countries have been taken over by the creditors, the bankers. And there was no choice but for all these countries to declare bankruptcy. In 1930, there was a world wide depression. If they had refused, the bankers would have totally collapsed their economies. The bankers "made them an offer they couldn't refuse."

The bankers said, "Look, you can do it the Easy way or the Hard way. Accept the bankruptcy and we'll let you out of the depression. If you don't your on your own."

So all the countries involved agreed to this blackmail, because they realized that the International Bankers had them by the tail.

The countries agreed to over several years pass legislation and statutes for implementing the Bankruptcy in favor of the international bankers. And this is what they did.

It would probably be correct to say that the key bankers were the Rothschild's and their agents, by way of the non-federal Federal Reserve Bank. Who the bankers are is immaterial. The fact remains that there is an International Bankruptcy and an International Conspiracy to cover it up.

An International creditor made the offer and the countries accepted the offer in order to continue, without a worldwide revolution, and to allow their politicians to remain in place. The countries were allowed to continue to operate, under the delusion of solvency, while in fact, they are totally bankrupt.

# 19
# The People-Snare

The Bankruptcy scheme was and is an extremely clever diabolical plan. These foreign bankers devised deceptive ways and means to con Americans into voluntarily declaring themselves to be "Citizens" and "Residents" of the corporate United States, whether they were or not. Remember, the corporate United States is bankrupt per private Public Policy agreement contract.

After American's had been tricked into claiming that they are "citizens" of the corporate United States, they were given a Social Security Number which tied them to certain "benefits" and "privileges." Then the bankers conned the employers to function as unpaid tax collectors to con their employees into filling out **W-4 intangible property gift forms** concerning their incomes and **1040 voluntary agreement contracts** that established their **"voluntary" indebtedness** to the banker creditors for all time.

If at any time they were to balk at this scheme because they don't like it, the real creditor does not have to make an appearance in court to declare the **"true nature and cause of the action"** that is being brought against the **so-called voluntary taxpayer** involved. He ends up dealing with an agency he doesn't understand.

The agency can simply grant itself immunity from prosecution because it is (without your knowledge and consent) administrating the bankruptcy which the government agreed to at the five year long Geneva Convention.

The court system never lets you put the original creditor on the courtroom stand, so you can ask him how he got attached to your back. The system is set up so that the creditor is protected and never has to make an appearance, and never has to produce "the law" that gave him the right to pledge you, your body, and your labor into indebtedness, bondage, and unknowing voluntary servitude.

Why? Because the 1930 Geneva agreement was perfected by Treaty, instead of by Legislation. The agreement came first, signed in secrecy, then Congress passed bankruptcy legislation to support the debt obligation required by the treaty.

Courts make decisions based on the new controlling admiralty law of bankruptcy.

**This has nothing to do with Constitutional rights. All cases brought into the courts are under the new bankruptcy law. They are bankruptcy cases cleverly disguised as Constitutional cases instead.**

# 20
# The Fraud

The members of the Supreme Court realized what was happening to them and the American system of law. The court was being asked to perform in creditor, debtor bankruptcy proceedings to benefit the banker creditors. The members of the Supreme Court said, *"No. We will not give you a bankruptcy proceeding decision that you can enforce against everyone; a decision not only in regard to Washington D.C. but having effect within the corporate governments of the individual states."*

This is fraud. It wouldn't have been fraud if the federal and state governments had declared bankruptcy and then told the people about it.

You and I are not the corporate government. The corporate government is a neutral zone known as the corporate capital of the corporate state. The government is where the corporate state exists as corporate headquarters. Corporate Washington D.C. is the seat of the corporate Federal Government. The capital of the corporate state is the seat of the corporate state government.

If the corporate Federal Government and her subsidiary corporate state governments want to join together and declare bankrupcy that is not fraud. That is corporate business. But when those two corporate entities declare bankruptcy and do not disclose this to you and me, and every other American, it *is* fraud (that they have so declared bankruptcy and not told us of it).

<u>In bankruptcy all debts are forgiven</u>.

But they do not disclose that their intention is to get you and me and every American to pledge to pay for their forgiven corporate debt to their corporate creditors. The corporate bankruptcy was the responsibility of the corporate state and the federal government, not the responsibility of the American people.

The corporate "United States" is a legal fiction that is distinct and separate from the private unenfranchized people of America. America and Americans were in existence prior to the creation of the corporate United States. The United States Inc. located its U.S. headquarters in Washington D.C.

The state territory called Virginia State gave land, something of tangible value, to the newly formed United States Corporation, and the United States Corporation agreed in the Constitutional contract to protect the individual States. But instead, because of the Corporate U.S. Bankruptcy, this corporate entity has enslaved the people and the states by deception, at the will of the foreign bankers with whom it is and has been doing business.

Our forefathers gave their lives, their property, and their sacred honor to prevent our enslavement. And yet today we are once again enslaved.

Private natural Americans have been tricked, deceived, and set-up to carry the perpetual debt of the corporate U.S. Inc. under bankruptcy laws. Every time an American appears in court, the corporate U.S. Bankruptcy is being administered against them without their knowledge and lawful consent. This is Fraud.

All corporate bankruptcy administration is done by "Public Policy", of, by, and for the Mother Corporate United States (U.S. Inc.).

# 21

# Public Policy Of Mother Corporation

The corporate bankruptcy is carried out under the public policy of the corporate United States in Washington D.C. The states use state public policy to carry out federal public policy in the states. Only public policy is being administered against Americans in the worldwide corporate courts of today.

The people of the world have been enslaved into corporate indebtedness.

It has become public policy for the American people to become voluntarily indebted to the International bankers of the world. All of the laws passed since 1938 are corporate public policy laws dealing only with corporate public policy.

Understand that U.S. corporate public policy is not an American public policy. The public policy of (belonging to) the United States corporation is not the policy of (belonging to) the Republic.

The *Erie v. Thompkins* case was a decision based upon public policy. All court decisions at any level since 1938 have been public policy decisions. All statutes, rules, regulations, and procedures that have been passed since then, civil or criminal, federal or state, have been passed to implement the public policy of bankruptcy.

Ever since 1933, when FDR came into office, public policy has been in force. He declared that it was the public policy of the U.S. government to call in all the gold and declare a banking holiday. It was the public policy of Washington D.C. (the federal government) to give government assistance to the people. Public policy operates the same within the states. All federal court decisions can only be handed down if the states support Federal public policy. The state legal systems must comport (be compatible) with the Federal legal system.

This is why, when people like us go to court without being represented by a lawyer, we throw a monkey-wrench into their corporate administrative proceedings. Why? Because all corporate public policy lawyers are pledged to up-hold public policy, which is the corporate U.S. administration of their corporate bankruptcy. This is why many if not all of our briefs are stamped, "THIS CASE IS NOT TO BE CITED IN ANY OTHER CASE AND IS NOT TO BE REPORTED IN ANY COURTS."

When we go in to defend ourselves or file a claim, we are not supporting the corporate bankruptcy administration and procedure. The arguments that we put forth pre-date 1938.

Before 1938, the law was not a public policy law. Today, the cases are decided under corporate public policy. Public policy exists to administer the bankruptcy for the benefit of the banker creditors and to protect the banker creditor.

Public policy allowed the creditor to say to the corporate legislatures, *"I want a law passed requiring my debtors to wear seat belts. Why? Because I want to be able to milk my debtors for the longest period of years possible."*

It doesn't behoove the creditor to allow all of his labor-producing debtors to die at an average age of 30 years. By having the consumer population live to retirement age, the bankers' lending, interest, penalties, increase, repayments, etc. on the entire funding and lending process would be more than doubled. (30 - 20 = 10, whereas 60 - 20 = 40; = 30 more years of indebtedness).

If the bankers can get people to live to an average age of seventy years, we are talking about 50 years of indebtedness, that they would be forced to pay back with interest.

The creditors, and their property and people, are considered to be well taken care of. The creditor doesn't want the population to decrease, unless that is, the people reach the maximum of the debt that they can carry and instead of paying off the creditor become a drain on the creditor. The creditor must then pay them to live and take care of them, or get rid of them.

The public policy of the corporate United States, and the counties and the cities, is that you must take care of these people. You must provide them with welfare, etc. Why? Because when you allow laws to be passed which say that the minorities must be cared for, the corporate legislature can say that it is public policy that the people want these people to be taken care of, and be given a chance to live, therefore we must raise taxes to fund these benefits, privileges and opportunities.

"Public" means, of and for the corporate Government. It does *not* mean, of and for the private people. It is *corporate* government policy. When they talk about public debt, they are talking about *corporate government debt* and you're the presumed pledge against this *corporate* created debt.

MY HOME IS MY CASTLE

## 22
# Your Signature

<u>Your signature is your most valuable personal property</u>.

Your property is *presumably* pledged for the rest of your life upon your signature. And your promise to perform is *presumably* pledged into perpetual debt.

The bankers don't even bother to go to court. They leave it up to the agencies to administer the public policy of corporate United States. It is the public policy of corporate agencies to bill you on your promise to perform. Then if you don't pay, they follow up on the public policy with a notice of default, and give you one more chance to pay. Then they proceed to sell your property at a tax auction sale.

They never go to court or appear in court to back up their claim against the mortgagee which is you.

So they put your property up for sale. At the tax sale, then average American Joe Doe bids on your property and wins the bid. Now, there is a procedure that he must go through step by step to establish. He is required to give you another chance. You have six months and a day to pay off the fines, etc., then your property is taken off default status and it is yours to continue to pay taxes on the next year.

Did any of your government-licensed and controlled teachers ever tell you that <u>your signature is your most valuable personal property</u>? Did any of your government teachers ever tell you that any time you sign any document, you should signe it **"without prejudice"** or with **"all rights reserved"** *above* your signature. Signing thusly means that you are reserving your God-given, unalienable rights, which cannot be transferred, and all other rights for which your forefathers died.

The Corporate U.S. Government provides, or at least pretends to provide for this reservation of rights under the Uniform Commercial Code, at UCC 1-207 and 1-103.

You need more information in this area. It is not in the best interest of the public schools of the corporate United States to teach you about their bankruptcy proceedings and that they have such a scheme to compel you into paying their debt. The "public" schools of the corporate United States are strictly designed for their corporate citizen/subjects, namely, the citizens of the "public" schools of the corporate United States.

Notice the emphases on being a "good" citizen. All the teachers and the students of the "public" schools of the corporate United States are trained to produce labor and material in exchange for valueless green paper called "money." It is not money, but functions *as money.* Lawful money must be backed by something of value.

The bankers take your labor, services, and material — meaning your homes, cars, farms, etc., — in exchange for their valueless corporate paper. This paper is backed only by the "full faith and confidence of the United States Government", the Mother Corporation.

# 23
# The Real Estate Snare

How do these bankers work this scheme in the area of Real Estate? These bankers have secured legislative concession that it is public policy that all land and property be pledged to the creditors in payment of the national (bankruptcy) debt which the creditor claims under the bankruptcy.

You or your parents have signed commercial instruments giving information and jurisdiction to the bankers through their agents. Such as, but not limited to, the following:

Social Security registration, use of your social security number, IRS forms, driver licenses, traffic citations, jury duty, voter registration, use of your address and zip code, U.S. postal service, deeds, mortgage applications, etc., etc. The bankers *then* use these instruments under the Uniform Commercial Code (UCC) as contractual agreements.

These documents are used as promissory contracts whereby you have promised to perform according to the contractual demands. This scheme involves you with the true creditor without your ever having become in contact with him. You are never told who the true creditor is. You are never told the **"true nature and cause"** of the paperwork you have signed.

Examine your real estate deed. You promised to pay taxes to the corporate government on property you originally acquired through a mortgage. But the corporate government never promised to pay taxes to the creditor. You did instead.

There is no mention in the mortgage or the deed of the **"true nature and cause of the action."**

Since you promised to perform, you get a bill for property taxes every year. The only way they can bill you for property or income taxes is through your own agreement to pay the tax. You *volunteered* to pay the tax. They *conned* you into promising to pay a property tax. When they send you a bill, they are coming against you for the performance of the promise you made to the creditor.

Now, the creditor appears to you as the local bank. But the bank has not loaned you anything. They have no credit to loan. There is a credit involved, but it is the credit of the International bankers. The international bankers are making you the supposed loan based upon the bankruptcy claim that they presume to have against you personally, and your property.

Now, let's say that you don't know that in bankruptcy all debts are forgiven. You are unaware of the remedies provided for you in the Uniform Commercial Code (UCC) whereby the UCC allows you to discharge your debts. To discharge the tax bill the county is presenting to you. So instead, you don't do or say anything. A couple of years go by, then all of a sudden you're being sent letters to pay up what is owed, or else your property will be taken from you after a certain period of time and put up for tax sale.

If you don't pay or discharge your tax bill and they contact you asking you to pay it and you don't, they will declare you in default. And based upon that default, as provided for in the UCC, they can sell your property, simply for the tax. (for the rent).

However, the county never goes into court to put into the record the identification of the real creditor, the International bankers. The county does not state the **"true nature and cause of the action"** against you. That it is a *bankruptcy* action, disguised as a *tax* action. Why? Because under bankruptcy, they have developed a legal procedure based upon your promise to pay.

They don't have to come to the court to get a court order authorizing the sale of your property. So the *real* creditor never makes an appearance in court. And you are denied your right to appear in court to challenge the creditor. To ask if he became the creditor under "public policy". To ask: *"If it is under "public policy", just what is the public policy that it is under? And how did you, as an international banker, become 'creditor' to me and everyone else in America?"*

They don't want you to ask the real creditor — the International bankers — to produce the documents upon which your personal debt was established. If they were forced to go into court, they would have to produce the deed or mortgage showing that you *knowingly, willingly,* and *voluntarily* promised to pay the U.S. corporate, public, national debt.

You did *not* knowingly, willingly, and voluntarily promise to pay any U.S. Corporate Bankruptcy obligation made in the 1930's.

This would expose their racket.

There was absolutely no debt connected to you until you agreed to it through their deception and fraud. The deception, in the broader sense, permeates throughout the educational system — and the news media and others — to sell you on the idea that you are an incorporated statutory "Citizen" and "Resident", strawman of the corporate United States.

MY HOME IS MY CASTLE

*"Ye shall know the truth, and the truth shall set you free."* — Christ Jesus at John 8:32.

Hardcore Redemption-In-Law: *Commercial Freedom And Release*
http://tinyurl.com/2fc6zej

Give Yourself Credit: *Money Doesn't Grow On Trees*
http://tinyurl.com/2epqjxw

Commercial Redemption: *The Hidden Truth*
http://tinyurl.com/yj4otn4

Oil Beneath Our Feet: *America's Energy Non-Crisis*
http://tinyurl.com/26vewuy

Untold History Of America: *Let The Truth Be Told*
http://tinyurl.com/y8hwvzr

New Beginning Study Course: *Connect The Dots
And See*
http://tinyurl.com/ybxdvgp

Monitions of a Mountain Man: *Manna, Money, & Me*
http://tinyurl.com/ygtkak8

Maine Street Miracle: *Saving Yourself And America*
http://tinyurl.com/yg9q8mm

Reclaim Your Sovereignty: *Take Back Your Christian
Name*
http://tinyurl.com/y8kuutb

Epistle to the Americans I: *What you don't
know about The Income Tax*
http://tinyurl.com/yfplutf

Epistle to the Americans II: *What you don't
know about American History*
http://tinyurl.com/yzme458

Epistle to the Americans III: *What you don't
know about Money*
http://tinyurl.com/yzuffbe